Life with No

W
o
r
d
s

Alby Lee Lewis

ISBN: 978-1-4834-5886-1 (sc)
ISBN: 978-1-4834-5887-8 (hc)
ISBN: 978-1-4834-5885-4 (e)

Library of Congress Control Number: 2016915749

Lulu Publishing Services rev. date: 10/28/2016

DEDICATION

In loving memory, I dedicate this book to my very good friend Frank, who studied side by side with me, hour upon hour, as we got through our struggle to learn to read. If ever one of us got a little tired or just didn't want to continue studying, the other would help keep it going. Frank passed away in July of 2015. We knew each other more than eight years. I still recall his perseverance and determination to get through our classes. We had good times, and I miss him.

CONTENTS

FOREWORD

It is clear that while reading words on a page has always been a struggle for Al Lewis, he was far from "illiterate." Al's ability to read the world around him (Freire and Macedo, 1987) and to write his own identity as a reader of people and the world allowed him to accomplish amazing things.

Al's life story is a remarkable account of someone who struggled not just with the inability to read words on the page, but it is of someone who struggled with hunger and homelessness and with having to navigate systems of inequity in order to survive. Yet his story is not just one of survival; it is a true success story. He was gainfully employed, married and had a child, retired at the age of 55, and accomplished all of this without being able to decode words and put them together to form sentences. However, he should have never been put in a position where he felt the need to hide and disguise his secret.

This account of Al's life is a success story, but it is also a call to action for those who have experiences similar to Al's and to educators who have, or will have, students like Al in their classrooms.

Every time Al Lewis, along with his wife, Bonnie, and daughter, Jackie, visited one of my Elementary Literacy or Secondary Content Literacy classes at North Central College to speak with aspiring teachers about how he navigated an education system and the workforce without learning how to read, the majority of my students were astounded. His wife, who always reminded us that she loved him, and that his reading issue was not what she saw when she looked at Al, supported Al as he navigated his adult life as a non-reader. Though she attempted to help him learn to read, Al explains that it would later take the expertise of a skilled teacher.

His visits were followed by discussions about how the system initially failed Al and what their role in education is in regard to developing readers. Invariably, at least a few students in my class would presume that Al's inability to read for so much of his life was a result of a time past and a broken system. However, as he spoke, students became comfortable sharing their own difficulties with reading and those of family members and friends. One student explained that she couldn't read until she moved to a new school in the fourth grade. Another explained that he couldn't read until he was tested and received services for dyslexia. Still another, through tears, explained that her brother, in his senior year of high school still found it nearly impossible to read a page of text.

While these students were raised in loving, caring homes and in education systems that were ripe with resources, they still struggled. The lessons they and their peers learned from Al and the conversations sparked by his visit far surpassed those I could share with them about the importance of teaching literacy skills, of helping students when they struggle, and of advocating for students.

Al had lived, persevered, and even flourished in a world in which he was not able to read. Although what he accomplished is a remarkable testament to his savvy and intelligence, living with his secret was a struggle and something he worked hard to hide and disguise. My students learned a lesson from Al that I tried to teach but could never drive home in the way he could.

I am elated that Al has written this book. Understanding his life story will undoubtedly serve as an inspiration and motivator for many. Reading this book will help future educators to better understand the responsibility they have to each of their students. It will also resonate with those who have had some of the same struggles Al has had and their family and friends, for they will understand that they are not alone and that there are resources and people who can assist them.

Through his own self-advocacy and the advocacy on the part of his daughter, a then aspiring future educator, Al did find the resources he needed to become a reader. With the loving support of his wife, Bonnie, he tackled adult literacy work with the same fervor he had once used to disguise his inability to read. His adult literacy teacher, Renai, assisted Al in accomplishing what after going through years of school and an entire career Al never thought was possible. He learned to read.

The reader can hear the cadence of Al's unique voice clearly throughout this book. As I read it, it was as though he was again speaking to us, to each of us, reminding us how important it is to be responsible for one another, and as teachers, to be accountable to our students.

Mary Beth Ressler, Ph.D.
Assistant Professor of Education
North Central College
Naperville, Illinois

PREFACE

Nowadays you cannot get away with not knowing how to read. It's a must. As an adult, it's never too late to start getting professional help so you can reach your goal. I hope my story will be of some inspiration to you.

This is a true story of a family of eight starting out in the 1940s in the city of Chicago and, in particular, one of the sons named Alby. This is my autobiography. Our family had many hardships, but we struggled through and tried to stay together. No one realized at first, but besides being hungry most of the time, I was having a problem that no one else in my family had. I lived with a secret that didn't become widely known until I was fifty-five. I was a guest on *The Oprah Winfrey Millennium Show* in 1999 and was proud (at that time) to tell the world that I had dyslexia all my life and now finally was coping much better than I ever thought possible.

It is a story of how, as a young boy, I was pushed through a school system where teachers did not recognize my incapability to pronounce or write letters or words.

Despite my issues, I was able to maintain my feelings of self-worth and keep a positive attitude through the years. It took some real planning on my part to navigate through so many situations that might have defeated someone else with similar problems. I believe my determination enabled me to succeed.

My story shows some of the sad realities and hardships I had to go through, but it also shows the humorous aspects of my life while growing up in a very poor and sometimes unstable environment. By telling my story, I am trying to give support and hope to others who have a hard time communicating through the written word. I hope to inspire others to step up, put aside their pride, and ask for help. We can do it.

ACKNOWLEDGMENTS

Being one of the lost boys for such a long time makes me realize the importance of all the people that helped me along the way. Those who listened to my cries for help and gave me direction and inspiration to keep going forward are the best teachers I have ever had in my life. There are five special teachers I need to acknowledge:

First teacher: Without my mom, Marie Lewis, and her guidance and strength in my poor younger years, I can't imagine where I would be today. Or maybe without her kind and gentle direction, I may not have even survived my childhood. She gave me the basics of life by which to live.

Second teacher: Having found my best friend, Bonnie, our getting married was a very positive step. We met in 1962 and were married in 1964. Her encouragement, understanding, and love have been the cornerstone of my life. With her help, we put together a story I hope will be inspirational to students as well as teachers. Bonnie has stood by me for a very long time and continues to do so.

Third teacher: Without our precious daughter, Jackie, there probably would not have been a turning point in my life. Because of her resourcefulness and determination to help her father achieve what she believed he could accomplish, which was to learn to read, she changed my life forever. Jackie got me back to school, and she continues to provide guidance. She was also very instrumental in the compiling and publishing of this book.

Fourth teacher: Renai Graham helped me accomplish what I never thought in a million years I would be able to do: read. For eight years, her patience and unrelenting attention to my struggle to understand the rules in the English language really astounded me. She is truly a remarkable teacher to have been able to get through to me and so many of my classmates.

Fifth teacher: My daughter, Jackie asked me to be a speaker at North Central College in Naperville, Illinois, when she was employed there. She asked me to speak to students who were studying to be elementary, middle, and high school teachers, and for me to try to relate to them how my experience was, growing up in the public school system, with my total inability to read. The head of the class was a very special person: Dr. Mary Beth Ressler, Ph.D., assistant professor of education. Dr. Ressler was also instrumental in the making of my book and wrote the foreword. I cannot thank her enough.

I am beyond fortunate to have been so lucky to have the love and encouragement of these wonderful ladies, who brought me into and moving along through this world. I'm thankful for all the good people I have met along the way who were kind and understanding to me. Today I am a strong and proud person because of all of them. I will continue going along.

INTRODUCTION

Words….. I was talking fine as I was growing up, so many years ago. Although my grammar was not the greatest, I had conversations with people all the time. It was those letters, the ABCs, that got me. I could recite the alphabet and sing the song like everyone else. The problem came when certain letters were put with other letters and it was now supposed to be a word.

How do you say *dog*? You don't say, "Dee-oh-gee." Why could I not understand that each letter has its own sound and some have two sounds, depending on the other letters around it. How crazy was that?!

I suppose I did okay in kindergarten, but the rest of my formal education was pretty much a flop. The teachers just put me in the back of the room. Some teachers must have thought I was stupid, uncooperative, or lazy. I didn't understand why I could not get those letters that are supposed to turn into words. I could not read anything.

CHAPTER 1
The Beginning

"*Well, I'll be*," said Warren Lewis after the birth of his sixth child at their home in Davis Junction, Illinois, a little town near Rockford, on Christmas Day 1940. Thus my name became ***Alby***.

My mom and dad were together during the Great Depression. They had lost their jobs and were struggling to get by. By the time I came along in 1940, I had three older brothers, Larry, Leroy, and Carl, and one sister, Ann. I would have had another sister by the name of Evelyn, but she caught a virus when she was just five years old and died before I was born. Two years after me came Norman, and then in 1944 came Ramona (Mona). All the Lewis children were born at home with the help of a midwife—except Mona, who was born in a hospital. We eventually moved from Davis Junction to Chicago.

My dad was basically a good man who tried to keep his family together and provide for it. He was our dad, who we looked up to and sometimes feared. It's unfortunate, but his biggest downfall was his dependence on alcohol. He was only in his late sixties when he died due to poor health.

Communication was not as good as I would have liked it to be, because there were so many of us. We all remember some bad times, but there were good times too. Sometimes life was very hard, but we all went through it together.

Our mom, however, was our go-to person for everything. She was our pillar of strength. When things got bad, she would help us all through it. Her motto was "Just get along." I didn't realize how many hardships our mom went through until I was older and could then understand and appreciate all she had done. She instilled positive thinking in all of us. We felt protected. She also gave us strength and guidance. Although Mom's life was filled with stress, she lived to be in her nineties, probably because of her kind and gentle nature and our love for her.

Despite all the extreme difficulties, disappointments, and pain we experienced, thanks to my parents we all turned out to be caring and responsible adults. My recollection of my family growing up together may not be the same as the recollections of the rest of my brothers and sisters, but I believe as a family we survived some tough times and helped one another through it.

My struggle with reading was and still is to this day a challenge for me after so many, many years. I hope that my story may be an inspiration to others.

In looking back, I wonder, what is the true meaning of *family*? I think it is a group of loving people joined together as a unit, where parents have fulfilled their dreams of having their own children, and the children feel loved and protected. Back in the old days, large families were the norm, especially when the parents had to work a farm. They needed all the extra hands they could get. We were pretty much city folk who had no farm to tend, but there were so many of us. It makes me wonder how parents can possibly control or take care of each child, emotionally and physically, when there are so many of them. We know it's not the child's fault or responsibility to control the number of family members. Who then is responsible?

I wouldn't give up any of my brothers and sisters for the world. But things may have been a little better for my parents, and for all of us, if they had not had so many children. I guess we were lucky we survived our upbringing. I always knew that if I ever got married someday, I would probably have one or maybe two children—no more.

CHAPTER 2
Apartments

Mom and Dad and their now seven children were evicted often, so we had to move around a lot. We had very little money. But I thought we had a pretty regular life. We played and slept but never really had enough to eat. There was no such thing as saying you didn't like what was being served for a meal. If you weren't quick enough, it would be gone in a flash, and you would go hungry.

We lived in various apartments, once in our car, and in different foster homes. Some of us also lived in juvenile detention. We carried on as best we could. I remember a fire in one of our apartments where we lived. I think one of my brothers caused it. The apartment was actually an empty store, but we had a roof over our heads. We were asked by the landlord to vacate one apartment because one of my brothers threw paint on a window. We had nowhere to stay except our car. It was awful.

In the early 1940s, our mom and dad put all our belongings into storage. It was everything we owned: clothing, photographs, furniture, dishes, towels, everything. When they went to retrieve our stuff, they found that all our items had been confiscated or sold. We never saw any of it again. We had nothing.

When the authorities found us all living in a car, we were all separated. I don't remember where my parents went. My two older brothers were sent to a detention institution for bad or homeless children, sometimes referred to as "an Audi Home for juveniles."

My younger brother, Norman, and my two sisters and I were sent to foster homes. One evening I went to bed, and the next morning, I found my clothes, which had been washed and folded, at the end of my bed. The dime I'd had in my pocket, which was my one worldly possession, was gone. I was so upset that I ran away. They found me and put me in the juvenile detention facility with my two older brothers. We were there for what seemed like a very long time. I think I was eight or nine years old. At least I was not alone.

Finally, my parents were able to get an apartment on Clark Street in Chicago. It was above a dry-cleaning store. In order to enter the apartment, we had to go around the back alley into a big parking lot, where we would climb the stairs one story above the cleaners.

In the winter, it was my job, along with my younger brother, to bring home the kerosene for our furnace. Norman and I had to walk about a mile round-trip in the bitter cold to get the five-gallon can of kerosene. It felt more like three or four miles. We never felt warm enough with our poor clothes, which were either hand-me-downs or old clothes from Goodwill stores. It wasn't easy growing up.

From the rooftop we could look over the side and see Clark Street. In the summertime, we would bring our mattresses out onto the roof to sleep, because it was so, so hot.

We never forgot that we had bedbugs and cockroaches. We used to get bitten by bedbugs all the time, and our resident cockroaches were on the kitchen floor, in the sink, and on the countertop. They would always scatter when we came into the kitchen. We actually kind of got used to our pets; it was our way of life. We and our cockroaches and bedbugs seemed like one big happy family. Sometimes we had a mouse problem, but we also had stray cats that were more than happy to be invited into our rooms. They caught the mice and went on their way. That worked out well.

Among our many pets was a dog we named Betty, a black and tan Doberman Pinscher my dad brought home one day. Unfortunately, my dad was not very nice to that dog. I don't know why we had her. If Betty didn't respond to my dad's commands immediately, he would kick her. Eventually, Betty would cower when she was with my dad.

One time, someone must have left our gate open, and Betty got out. Our next-door neighbors had a rabbit. Well, the little girl who owned that rabbit must have not put him in his cage, because Betty brought the (dead) rabbit home. My brother, Carl, said, "Oh, now we're in trouble." So we boys cleaned up the rabbit and put it back in its cage, hoping they would think the rabbit had experienced a heart attack. It didn't take the girl very long to realize her pet was dead. And we were definitely suspects.

Betty was not an animal we could play with. She quite often would bite us if we startled her. After she had a litter of nine puppies, they disappeared, and so did Betty. That was not a good memory.

There were no screens in the windows, so mosquitoes and other flying pests became a constant nuisance in warmer weather. The hot summer nights were sometimes unbearable. The girls' bedroom was small, about the size of a large closet.

One time we had a bat attack. My older sister got a bat tangled in her hair. With much screaming and jumping around, we finally got it out of her hair. Thank goodness that didn't happen too often. What a life!

As I think back about Clark Street, I see that so much has changed. Now there are many high-rise apartments and condominiums on Clark Street. It's amazing we lived through all the stuff that happened to us in that neighborhood. I'd seen so many street fights and gang leaders fighting. On one occasion, a group of tough guys surrounded me. I was terrified, but, just in time, the police came and broke it up. I was lucky again.

CHAPTER 3
Doctor Mom

Only minor injuries happened to me during my adolescence. Kids were always trying to steal my bike. I didn't have to fight, because I rode away with such great speed, I surprised myself.

My brothers would pick on me, too, of course. One time I came home and asked Mom to look at the back of my head. She pulled out a fork that my brother Carl had thrown at me just for fun. She just wiped my head off and put a bandage on it.

Another time, my nose got broken, but I'm not sure when. It might have been the time I jumped off a one-story building or during one of those fights I somehow got pushed into. We kept Mom very busy.

Mom was very good at fixing us up. One time I was knocked down pretty hard by the tough guys down the alley, and my skull was cracked. Mom pushed it together and put bandages on my head. That was how it was then: no money, no stitches. Things just got taped up. The lead pencil injection some guy at school gave me left a mark in my leg, which I still have.

When I was about nine years old, a terrible thing happened in the alley. Someone threw a knife and struck me in my back. I got scared and ran home and waited for my mother to come home. She just taped it up and said I was okay.

In the summertime, I believe, we were in the back parking lot, playing with two or three friends, when a man approached us who seemed to be drunk and not a very nice person. We felt this man was going to hurt us. I happened to have an empty can in my hand, and because he looked like he was going to attack me, I put my fist into the can, swung it, and hit him in face. We all ran, and when we came back, we were so glad he was gone.

The area we lived in was not very nice at all. It's amazing that just two blocks away from our apartment the neighborhood was very nice, with residents who I'm sure were rich.

My brother Norman and I and some friends would go to a five-story apartment building next door to where we lived. In order to empty the garbage container each week, they had a pulley system that hung over the railing. They would lower the garbage in very large containers to the main floor.

I would hold the rope and swing across to the stairs to my apartment. One day, the rope snapped, and I fell one story to the porch below. Believe me, that was the last time I did that. It hurt so much. I was sure that I broke my back. When I got home, my mother looked at it and told me to lie down and rest. The next day, I felt a little better. I guess I didn't break my back after all. It's amazing how we fixed things and avoided seeing a doctor. We really couldn't, because we had no insurance and very little money.

Another time, a fire broke out at an antique shop a half a block away. My brother and I went over there, and we noticed five swords. No one was looking, and in the chaos, we took the swords. We knew it was wrong, but we did it anyway. I don't remember, but we probably sold or traded them for something.

One day we found a handgun in a garbage can and brought it home to our father. We were lucky that we didn't get shot, because the gun was loaded. My father probably sold the gun so we could eat, and I'm sure he bought alcohol for himself.

My mother worked outside the home to help out. My dad worked, but he didn't go out a lot. We were sure he was an alcoholic. He missed a lot of work. When he got angry with us, he sometimes hit us. One summer I had severe sunburn, and my dad hit my back. I know he knew I had a bad burn, but I don't think he cared. He just said to me, "You were not good." I don't remember what it was that I did wrong.

My younger sister, Mona, fell against the glass cabinet in our house and got a huge cut in her leg. Our jaws dropped, because we knew it was very serious. My other sister, Ann, came into the room and yelled for me and my little brother to get towels. We all tried to stop the bleeding, waiting for either our mother or father to come home from work.

Finally, Dad arrived. When he picked Mona up, she fainted, and Ann screamed. It was quite a frightening experience for all of us. Mona ended up getting fifteen stitches, but she was okay. Unlike all us other kids, Mona was the only one born in a hospital and probably the first to be treated by a doctor, instead of just getting a bandage.

We didn't find out until many years later that having been born in a hospital was not such a blessing. Apparently the use of forceps to deliver Mona had caused damage to the left side of her brain. At age twenty-five, Mona had her first grand mal epileptic seizure while in a doctor's office. It was determined that she had been experiencing petite mal seizures all her life.

Up until the time Mona was diagnosed, she didn't realize that these feelings she had, which sometimes coincided with episodes of déjà vu, were because of a treatable condition. She thought she could see into the future, and she was afraid that she was a witch. Mona had another grand mal seizure when she was at work. She went into a coma for fourteen hours before coming to.

With proper medication, the seizures have been under control for quite some time. It's amazing our parents never knew their daughter was going through such a rough time. How unfortunate little children are not always protected and are left with scary thoughts. When, if ever, are we all really safe?

When I was about ten years old, my brother and I and a couple friends would go to Lincoln Park on the east side of Chicago. We would ride our bikes, and a couple times we had to speed away, because we were chased by a group of tough guys. They always tried to take our bikes, so we went pretty fast. Thank the Lord, they never caught us.

I built my bike from spare parts, which I probably stole or found, and I was not about to let my bike go. My brother and I were both quite good bike riders, so we always managed to get away. We could do wheelies and go very fast. This was one of the exciting things in my life.

There were some crazy things that happened. One time I held a broken beer bottle behind my brother Norm's back, pretending I was going to stab him. As I pressed the sharp end to his body, I was supposed to let the bottle slide through my hand just as a joke. But it didn't slide, and I stabbed my brother. His back was full of blood, so Doctor Mom cleaned the wound, pushed the skin together, and taped it up.

Because we moved around so much, very few photos of our family existed. I was able to hang on to a few of them. I believe I was eight years old in both these pictures. The first picture is me and a friend from school. He helped me by not letting other boys push me around. I was so glad he was my friend.

Al (right) with school friend

The second picture shows us with a neighbor and his dad. I'm standing on the dad's right side. My little brother

Norman is on the other side, and my older brother Carl is to Norman's left.

Al and brothers Norman and Carl

CHAPTER 4
Shopping

I remember all of us going with our mother to a popular thrift store. We walked around looking at shoes and things. Since our mother had no money, she would tell us to try on shoes and then put our old shoes on the rack. I know that was a terrible example, but it was that or no shoes. We then walked out of the store. We did our shopping this way quite often.

We children also traveled around in a small group. While in a dime store, my older sister and brothers would quite often slip things into a bag I was carrying, and I would just walk out the door. This is how we did our Christmas shopping. We also did some other trading at the Goodwill store. We knew it was wrong, but what else could we do?

We got caught stealing cheese one time. I was with my little brother and little sister. When the owner asked why we stole the cheese, Mona said, "Because we're hungry." The owner said that we should have told him that, and he would

19

have given us the cheese. We were frightened and thought he might call the police. But he was a very nice man, and he let us go. I promised I would never steal again.

When I was around seven or eight years old, my other older brother, Larry, had a job. After work, he would bring a pint of ice cream home once in a while. He sat there in front of all of us kids eating his ice cream and never shared it with us. We all thought that was so mean of him. And to this day, I still tease him about it.

Larry sometimes would grab me very hard by the back of my neck. My only defense after struggling to get loose was to run away. I was much faster than all of them, so I did have that advantage. My older brothers were not so nice to their younger sibling at times.

CHAPTER 5
Happiness

I always made a point to try to be happy. The things I did on a daily basis, like going to school, talking to people, and having a good time, were important. I knew things were not right with me, but I wasn't sure what the problem was. I used to make a point to talk to as many people as I could.

There was a problem with my ability to learn to read, but we didn't talk about it. It seemed that we just took it for granted that everything was okay. My mother always said that I was just a little different.

There were so many other things to do when I was younger, and a lot of it didn't involve reading. I tried to get along with everybody, and I made it a point to be happy. My mother always told me to just get along with everybody and everything would be all right. She said it is always easier that way.

As I started getting a little older, some situations seemed to be getting a little harder. I was no longer this little boy, running around, playing games, or just relaxing. I had some chores I had to do but really not too many responsibilities—not even homework. I think they stopped giving me homework at school because they knew I wasn't going to be able to do it anyway.

But no matter what situation I got into, I was always careful. I usually tried not to worry about anything. I looked at life like this: whatever I do, make it fun. I still think that way. Even to this day, I find myself asking the group of people I'm with, "Is everybody happy?" It just comes out.

When times were bad, like when there was no food or no heat, I just tried not to think about it. Whatever the situation was, it made me feel good in a way because I always managed somehow to get around it. But who was I kidding? I knew I was not normal, because I did have a real problem. I could not understand the concept of reading those so-called "words." No one in my family took my problem very seriously either.

CHAPTER 6
Early School

And Then There was SchOOL

We now lived in Chicago. I really don't remember kindergarten or much of the next eleven years in the Chicago school system where I spent time sitting at a desk in the back of the room. I'm sure the teachers had determined that I was just slow or lazy, or both. Or did they think I was just a troublemaker? I didn't know. Words made no sense to me. No matter how the letters were presented to me, nothing clicked.

Was I crazy? My sisters and brothers didn't seem to have too much of a problem. My mom tried to help. She had been a schoolteacher before marrying my dad. She had taught at a little one-room schoolhouse near Rockford. I believe she got back and forth by horse and buggy.

I had to be in school; it was the law. My dad didn't seem concerned about my reading difficulties, and my mom would just encourage me to be positive and try harder.

Because they said I was not a very smart boy, I was sent to an ungraded school called Franklin Elementary School. Kids of all ages were in the same classroom, and teachers tried to help us all to learn.

My brothers and sisters went to another nearby school, and we had to walk to and from our schools every day. There was no school bus service, and we certainly did not have money for public transportation. No matter what the weather was, we had to walk. It was some two to three miles each way. It wasn't easy.

Two of my brothers seemed to have some difficulty reading, but their problem didn't seem as bad as mine. I couldn't read, but no one ever talked about it, for some reason. I was very embarrassed about my inability to read, so I didn't want to talk about it either. I recall watching my father looking at a newspaper. I was never sure he actually was reading anything. In all my life at home, he never read anything to me or to anyone else. I don't understand why my mother and father didn't help me more. So, you learn how to get along and try to be happy.

I recall a class picture one year. I really stood out because I was the only white person in the school. I was able to participate in some of the classes, but I would never earn a passing grade in anything that involved reading. I was not the only one with problems. It was quite clear other kids in my class had difficulty with reading and math.

Being in the public school system in Chicago was a little rough. I learned to protect myself by being able to talk my way out of situations that were not pleasant. It seemed that some guys always wanted to beat me up. I made friends with some of the tough guys; one in particular I thank to this day because he was like a bodyguard to me. He was a really big guy and stood up for me. I have a very old photo of him and me, shown earlier in this book.

I started school when I was six. I was very perplexed because the classes in my school were mostly comprised of African-American students. Even though I knew I could not read, I wondered why I was in that school. The teachers also knew I couldn't read, but they did nothing about it.

School was no fun, but I looked forward to my gym classes and playing baseball outside during our lunch break and after school. I became a crossing guard, and I was very proud of that. I wore a white belt around my waist and my shoulder. I was usually late in getting back into the classroom because of my crossing job, but the teacher never said anything about being late. I just went to the back of the room and pretended to be working on something.

When I was nine years old, some guy stabbed me in my leg with a pencil. Another time at school, I was knocked across the room, and I hit my head on a wall. Nobody came forward to help me until finally someone put a bandage on my head and sent me home. My mother looked at it, taped it up, and sent me on my way.

I always sat toward the back of the classroom so I would not be noticed, and I wasn't. The teacher paid little attention to me. I don't recall anyone being asked to stand up and read whole sentences, and I thought that was normal. After a while, it was not that uncomfortable to be in the classroom. I knew so many of us had difficulty; it was not just me. It was the same with math. If I had to read the problem—well, I was lost.

Sometimes I felt very frustrated and would say to my mother, "Why me?" She would always say, "Just get along with everybody, and everything will just be okay." She always said everyone assumes that everybody knows how to read, so no one talks about it; so I didn't either. I didn't like it, but what could I have done about it?

I liked being part of the drum and bugle corps, which was one of the programs they offered in the school. I was eight years old. I played the drums quite well, I thought, even though I didn't read music; a lot of it was memorization. This was very exciting to me because there was really nothing else I could do in school, except talk. I was able to go into the band room a little earlier than the other kids, so I could practice. When we were all playing, I listened and just followed what they did, and I practiced over and over every chance I could get. I seemed to catch on fast.

Being part of the band really made me feel like I was part of something big and like I really did have a purpose being in school. I was very proud of my accomplishment. I was asked once to do a drum solo. I was very nervous, but I believe I did perform pretty well. That's when I felt that I had some good qualities, even if I couldn't read. So I knew I had to figure out the best way I could do interesting things that didn't involve reading.

After summer break, I came back to school. I was still eight years old, and nothing had changed. For me, reading was not happening. I don't believe the teachers in my classrooms understood or even cared that I had this problem. Some of the teachers actually got upset that I was not understanding and doing as well as some other students. There were not many students that did well, so I was not alone. At times I would sit there in the classroom and stare at the stuff they gave me to read. Looking at the papers, all I saw were just letters, no sounds, no sense to it at all. Maybe I couldn't concentrate because I was tired or hungry or cold. I don't know.

My inability to read forced me to memorize the words I heard as much as I possibly could. I did remember how to spell my name. I kept my address on a slip of paper in my pocket, just in case. Anything important had to be written down and kept in my pocket. Thinking back, it was amazing that I could get away with this secret.

By the time I was fifteen, I had accepted the fact that I had a real problem that nobody cared to solve or talk about. I know I was not the only kid that had this problem. Like me, so many kids were heading down the same difficult road. What else could we do? I never graduated. It was an ungraded school, so everyone had to do their time before being released to the world.

I sat in the back of the many classrooms until the age of sixteen and was then sent to a trade school. I learned in the machine shop to operate a lathe and other machines, which I enjoyed.

CHAPTER Working 7

I had to contribute to the family income. We all did. My mom went back to work after we were all in school. My father drank, sometimes to excess, and some days we were afraid to come home. Around age seven, I started shining shoes and delivering newspapers to do my part in bringing home some money.

I had a great idea, which I did for a while. I would buy some newspapers and then sell them for a profit. My best customers were in restaurants and especially in taverns. I soon discovered that the more the customers in taverns drank, the more they tipped. But it was really a little scary being in there. That wasn't an easy job, but I knew I had to come home with some money.

Another way we made some money was fishing in the Lincoln Park Lagoon. I don't remember where we got them, but Norman and I had fishing rods. We caught these big carp fish. We didn't need bait—just a big hook to snag them. We never brought them home, because Mom said they were dirty garbage-eating fish. So we were able to sell them to the local fisherman.

There was another source of income that all kids had: trick-or-treating! To get a little more treats, we would start the day before Halloween (it was called "beggars night"). On Halloween, we would start as soon as we could and go into the evening until people stopped answering the doors. Going house to house was fun, and we got the usual candy. But when we were able to sneak into the apartment buildings where the rich people lived, we usually got money instead of candy. I don't think they expected any kids to get into the buildings. But sometimes, after all our hard work, some bigger guy would come along and take our loot.

When Norman and I were able to collect a little money, we would go to the neighborhood Chinese restaurant and buy a bowl of rice with gravy over it. That was just heaven.

Not having money was such a nuisance. We had to steal to get anything. When I was about thirteen or fourteen, I worked part time at a horse stable during summer break. It was nice to work with horses, and I got to know the boss, which also helped. When I came home, everyone said I smelled like a horse and they avoided me until the odor went away. We had one bathtub (no shower), and if it was not my designated turn, I just had to wait.

The stable I worked at was Lake Shore Academy, and I got to know the owner very well. I was a stable boy, and after a few months, I got to know the horses by name. I'd memorize the names and identified them by just the first letter I saw above each stall. Besides working in the stalls, my boss asked me to work behind the counter and take messages. I agreed, but knowing I could not write down a message, I asked the person to call back when the manager returned.

When people came in to rent a horse and I was in the office instead of in the stable, I would ask them if they had a preference from the list of horses, then asked them to write their name after the horse's name. I was so grateful when people wrote these things down like I asked. They never knew I was not able to do it. This worked out very well.

Part of my job was putting saddles on the horses that were being sent downstairs for the riders. When each horse was saddled, I would direct the horse to the ramp, and it would run downstairs. I would help people get on the horses, and then I adjusted the stirrups. Some people needed to be shown how to hold the reins. That's what I did, day after day. It wasn't so hard, and I was happy. Times like that, I sat back and said, "I can do this."

I also rode the horses from time to time, but not too often, because they made me pay. I tried riding bareback. I didn't like it, because I quite often fell off. That was not fun. Occasionally, they let me ride for free. I really think it was because some horses needed to be exercised that day, but that was good for me too.

I always looked forward to horseback riding on Friday nights. A bunch of friends and other people and I would go out on the trail in Lincoln Park, so I got to know more people. I really enjoyed riding, especially in a full gallop. I liked to stay in the back of the group; when they started to go faster, I would go even faster and catch up with the first horse. That was fun, and it made me feel quite good. I always wanted to go faster.

That's when I realized that I could do a lot of things without knowing how to read. It wasn't always easy, but I always managed to get through it.

A couple of times my younger brother joined me on a trail ride. It was great fun to race against each other. Norm was a little rough on his horses, I thought. If they wouldn't do what he directed them to do, he would hit them with a stick or whack them behind their ears.

The riding academy held horse shows for the public outdoors in Lincoln Park. Twice I was asked to help out. Horses were brought in from many places. These were special, multi-gaited and, I'm sure, very expensive animals. It was my job to be in charge of them. It was very scary to hold on to five or six high spirited horses at one time. I was always glad when it was over. But you know what? I thought I did great!

Later in life, I returned to horseback -riding. It is a great sport. But back then, after being bitten, stepped on, and bucked off horses many times, I needed a break. Sometimes a horse I was riding would get startled and shy to one side, and there I would be, on the ground again. I decided to stop riding before I got seriously hurt. So that was my riding experience when I was younger. It was fun, but I'd had enough of horses.

When I was about fifteen years old, I worked in a small store called Pleasing Food Store, where I delivered groceries. It was across the street from where we lived on Clark Street. I made deliveries on a bicycle with a big basket. Because of all my past bicycle riding, I was the best and fastest bicycle delivery person. I recognized names of streets by memorizing the order in which the letters were placed.

Making deliveries to the apartment buildings was a little more difficult because I had to search all the names next to each bell, letter by letter, until I found a match. I was in trouble when there was no name by the bell. I'd have to ring the bell and ask if they were the person who ordered groceries. Then I would have to spell the name, because there was no way I could guess how to pronounce it. After a while, I would memorize the names and addresses of the good tippers. When I delivered groceries to houses, it was easier, because there were no names to read.

My delivery area was Lake Shore Drive, the Gold Coast, and other affluent areas. It was very hard work, especially when it was raining and during bad winter weather. I had to make deliveries, no matter what. If the tips had been better, that would have made it easier.

My boss would sometimes read the names and addresses to me before I started my route. When I made deliveries in the snow, I sometimes fell and some items got destroyed or two orders got mixed up. Then I had to return to the store so they could put the orders back together. I really despised winter. The cold, snowy weather forced me to ride my bike in the street, where I felt very much in danger. But that was my job.

Although they knew it was illegal for me to deliver liquor because I was underage, they expected me to do it anyway. They trusted me completely and knew I did not want anything to do with liquor. That's because my dad drank excessively and became a person I did not like. I never would want to be like that.

One day some customers the owner did not know made a request for a liquor delivery. He was a little suspicious. He thought I was streetwise and that I knew one gang in the area, so he asked me to make the delivery. He told me that if there was any problem, I should bring the delivery back.

It happened that I did know the customers and that they were underage. They also recognized me, and amazingly, I talked my way out of turning over the delivery to them. I just could not give it to them, and I'm thankful to this day I made it out of there alive and returned the liquor to the store. I asked my boss to never ask me to deliver liquor again.

Many problems were attached to that job. One day I was out there doing my job when a police officer approached me and questioned me about my whereabouts a couple of hours before. He had a description of a boy who robbed a woman on the street, and he said I fit the description.

I was terrified and feared I would go to jail because I could not prove it was not me. He took me over to his squad car where the woman was sitting. She looked at me carefully and then told the police I was not the one. Thank you, Lord. Saved again.

I had other duties working in the store, like sweeping, restocking shelves, even working in the meat department. They decided it was not a good idea for me to work with the butchers, because I almost took off a finger. It also wasn't good when I was asked to answer the phone and take orders. Of course, I could no way in the world do that. I don't remember all my excuses, but eventually they stopped asking. I would never have taken anything from them. They were very good to my brother and sister and me, and sometimes they even gave us food to eat.

Norman came to work for Pleasing Food Store about a year after I started. My little sister Mona eventually also started working there as a bookkeeper at age sixteen. She stayed with them until she retired, somewhere around the year 2005.

I finally quit school at sixteen. I had had enough of that nonsense. I remember just before the end of my school confinement, a teacher said to me, in all seriousness, "Al, you are probably going to have trouble out there. Good luck." Those words stayed with me for a very long time.

I went to what was known as a continuation school for one year, where I took machine shop and learned how to run some machines. I actually made things out of plastic and steel, like small containers. It felt like a bit of an accomplishment. Best of all, I thought it was so cool that I did this without having to read anything!

It was now time for the real job world, out there where written words had absolutely no meaning to me. With much practice, I could memorize the letter configurations in some words I really had to know. Sometimes I got them right.

My first job was at a company in Chicago that made contact lenses. The written application was not an issue. My older brother Carl worked there, and he got me in. I polished lenses, and mostly I dealt with numbers and gauges that read the prescriptions of the lenses. There were no word issues, and I worked there in 1958 and 1959.

I felt I was getting good at what I was doing, and it seemed more responsibility was about to come my way. But that, of course, would involve reading. I started getting very nervous about that, and I had to move on. It was a fun job, but I had to make a change.

When I was about nineteen years old, I got another job with my brother Carl, working with concrete. This was a very hard job. No application was needed, as Carl had connections. That job didn't last long. It was definitely not what I wanted to do; the work was much too hard.

That same year, my father got me a job at a company that made parts for boats. I lucked out and didn't have to fill out a form, because my dad took care of that. He worked there as a polisher on a buffing machine. He lost a thumb on one of those machines, and luckily he was able to continue working there.

I can't say working with my dad was what I wanted, but I needed the job. I started working assembling parts for boats. I learned to operate a drill press, assemble parts, and pack and ship products. I learned by watching others do a job and, then copying their moves. If instructions had to be read, I had to get around it somehow. I might have said, "I can't quite make that out" or "Sure, I'll get to that later." I made it a point to socialize with others, especially the bosses. I think they liked me, and they let some things slide.

I worked with my dad at that company for about one year. But I thought I could do better. When I finally got my driver's license (and that's a long story), I no longer had to depend on my dad or my brother to drive me to and from work, and public transportation was too expensive. I asked around about other facilities that made boat parts, now that I felt I was experienced in that field. I was referred to a manufacturer.

I went there and was so grateful I was able to take the application home to fill out. Yes! I got my mom to help me.

I got the job and picked up on it pretty fast. I made lots of friends and got to know the company foreman very well. In addition to the drill press, I learned how to use a milling machine and a lathe, and I assembled headlights and various parts for boats. The job did not pay very well, but I made lots of friends.

My company had me help set up a display for boat hardware at McCormack Place in Chicago. The serious problem was that I had to drive there. Not being able to read any street signs made it pretty darn hard. I got through it somehow. The job was a great experience; the driving was a nightmare!

So, there I was, twenty-one years old, and I was still working in a low-paying job in a factory, assembling boat parts. I knew there must be something better out there.

CHAPTER 8
Driving

When I was sixteen, my brother Carl taught me how to drive his car. It was a 1949 manual-shift Ford. He let me practice now and then.

Age twenty-one came along, and Dad took me for my first driver's license test. I failed the written test. Carl offered to let me use his car for a second test to get my license. He knew I had a problem with reading, and that I probably would not pass the written test again. He was able to bribe someone with thirty dollars to fill out the written test for me. I just signed the form. The actual driving test was no problem. I had my license!

I finally bought my first car when I was twenty-one, a 1955 Ford. But then there was a slight problem with getting around: street names and addresses. Street signs had a group of those funny-looking symbols (letters) that meant—WHAT? It was quite a challenge, but my new independence made me feel so happy. Think of the possibilities. I could drive anywhere, I could drive to work instead of taking public transportation, and most importantly, I could now take girls out. I was sure they would help me out with addresses. I had such freedom!

Of the few pictures that exist of me, this one was taken November of 1961 when I finally turned that all-important age of twenty-one.

Al at twenty-one

Now that I could drive, getting around was pretty much done by memory. I had to rely on landmarks to identify where

I was. It took a little while, but I amazingly managed to find a location more than once. It was great.

The next time I was required to take the written driver's test was when I was fifty-eight. I picked up one of the Rules of the Road, studied it, and passed the written test. I asked if I had gotten all the questions right and was told that I passed. But I said it was important to me to know if I got *all* the questions right? Finally, she said, "Yes, 100 percent right." This made me feel extremely good. The reason I was able to accomplish passing this test was because when I was fifty-five, a great change had taken place in my life, which I will explain later.

The way people treat you is so important. All this hiding in the past, trying to conceal that I had a problem, was so frustrating. I needed to know when I had done a good job. Later on in life, because my secret was out, I took on some situations a little differently. For example, I had to go to the doctor's office, and they gave me a form to fill out. I told them I do have a problem because I have dyslexia and that I would fill out the form as best as I could. When I handed the form back to the receptionist, she said I did a great job.

Now I think, *All those years I could have asked people for help.* My shame had held me back, so I never realized how kind and concerned most people are.

CHAPTER 9
Marriage

I didn't have a lot of girlfriends back then. I was kind of skinny and my teeth stuck out, and I didn't have much self-confidence. There were fun things to do like roller-skating, bowling, driving cars, and seeing girls. None of these required looking at useless words. I had no problem with the spoken word.

Having a car made such a big difference. I got to meet a lot of new friends. I thought I was extremely good at roller-skating and I was even thinking of skating professionally. That never happened.

One evening back in early 1962 at the Riverview Roller rink, I met a girl named Bonnie. She enjoyed skating and was pretty good, but not great. I asked her to skate, and we did. I drove her home that evening, and we starting dating regularly. Bonnie graduated from high school in 1963.

We had been going out together for about a year and a half when, for some reason, we broke up for a short while. She told me later it had nothing to do with my reading problem; but rather, it was just a crucial time in her life for decisions. She had just graduated high school. Isn't she supposed to go to college? She wasn't sure about it. She and I had a very close relationship, and I think she was feeling a little unsure and needed some space. In a relatively short time, though, we both realized how much we missed each other and decided to get back together.

It was time for the big question. I can't believe it, but I actually got down on one knee and asked her if she would marry me. I didn't buy a ring ahead of time, though. What would I do if she said no? But she did say yes, and I was very happy.

I guess Bonnie was a bit of an old-fashioned girl. After accepting my marriage proposal, she said it would only be proper for me to ask her father for her hand in marriage. Wow! But it wasn't so bad. Her father said, "Of course you can have her hand in marriage, and all the rest, too." We just laughed.

This was a very good beginning. Bonnie and I could leave our present homes and live independent of our parents. We both had jobs, and life would be good. I must admit that finally getting away from my parents, especially my dad, and the whole living-at-home experience was very much a part of my decision to get married. It was time, and fortunately I had found the right girl.

I brought Bonnie to meet my family, and they liked her. After we were officially engaged with a ring that we both picked out, we were again at my parents' home. Bonnie told me that my mom took her to the side and asked if she was aware that I had a reading problem. Bonnie said yes she was, but that we'd get through it okay. I don't remember when she first noticed I had an issue with words. I might have told her that I had this problem and we needed to talk about it. She was very understanding, and I felt very good about that.

We were very happy. My family was brought up in the Lutheran religion. Bonnie was brought up as a Catholic, so she needed to be married in the Catholic Church. This meant I had to go to counseling. It wasn't too bad. I don't recall having to read anything. But one of the subjects brought up was birth control. We told the priest we understood the church's rules on the subject. Bonnie and I had discussed having children, of course. She was one of six children and, like me, agreed not to have too many kids—maybe one or two. In the back of my mind, I always feared that any child of mine would have the same problem I did, but Bonnie assured me that the possibility of that happening was slim to none.

She wanted a September wedding, because she loves the fall season. We looked around for halls to have the reception, and some were very expensive. My mom belonged to a club and was able to get us use of a hall. It was nice enough, and the dinner was about seven dollars per person. (Things cost a little less back in those days.) We could handle that. One of the dates that were available was Saturday, July 11. That was close enough, so we chose that date. It was 1964.

Al and Bonnie on their wedding day

After the wedding, we drove to our two-room apartment on Wrightwood Street in Chicago. I almost forgot to carry her over the threshold when entering our new home for the first time as Mr. and Mrs. Lewis. We were so tired we managed to open all our envelopes from the wedding then pass out from exhaustion. I was twenty-four, and Bonnie was nineteen. We both felt that we could handle anything. We both had jobs, and our rent was sixty dollars a month. We were doing okay.

Then, of course, it was time to go on a honeymoon. We made no plans ahead of time. We figured we would just go, and everything would fall into place. It didn't matter; we were in love and had each other. Our car was an old 1949 Plymouth, which broke down somewhere along the way to our destination, the Wisconsin Dells. We never did find the Dells, and we were so tired we decided to spend the night in Milwaukee. We went to dinner and a show. The show was *It's a Mad Mad Mad Mad World*. We decided we'd have as much fun back home at our lovely apartment as we were having there.

We had what was called a "garden apartment." We had purchased a bedroom set. The rest of our furniture consisted of two old end tables with two lamps and a wooden kitchen table with two chairs, all of which were donated by either family or friends.

Bonnie was working at Sears Roebuck on Homan Avenue then. She had a secretarial position in the hardware department in the steno pool. She took the bus to and from work. We stayed at that apartment for just nine months. We had to sublet because we couldn't take it any longer. We didn't have any water problems, but the water and heating pipes for the building were right over our heads, and quite often the pipes banged very noisily. I think the last straw for Bonnie was when she put on her shoes to leave for work one morning and immediately pulled her foot out. Out came a big water bug. She said, "That's it."

We were able to find another apartment on Altgeld Street, not too far from our first apartment. We didn't have very much, so it was an easy move. Compared to our first apartment, it was extremely nice. We were on the second floor of a two-story brick building. We had a living room, bedroom, dining room, kitchen, bath, a little windowed patio, a pantry, and a back porch. Perfect. The apartment also had a beautiful built-in fireplace. It did not work, but that was okay; it looked nice. The rent was ninety dollars a month, but it was worth it. The entire building had a one-car garage that, unbelievably, was available to us. This was the best place to live I'd ever had in my entire life.

Still my reading issue went on. Bonnie tried to help me learn to read. It was tough. We bought a kit called "Hooked on Phonics" because I had no idea what the word phonics meant and no idea what any of the letters sounded like. I got a little better, but then it just went to the wayside.

Things were improving. I got the hang of my job by watching and learning and talking to people. Sometimes I had to write something and had no clue how to spell anything. I recall once I was not feeling well at work and needed to leave. I had to call Bonnie and have her spell the words to me to fill out the required form.

Things were "just going along" (my mom's favorite expression). We had been married for five years when we started talking about starting a family. I was not so sure it was a good idea. Again, I was afraid the child would have the same affliction I have. Bonnie and I talked at length. She told me she was so sure my reading problem would not be transferred to our child; our child would be very normal.

We thought my problem was possibly because I was born at home with no doctor present, so there might have been a slight shortage of oxygen during the birthing process, which could have caused it. Bonnie believed that having a problem with reading was in no way an indication of a lack of intelligence in me. She said I was one of most intelligent, kind, and caring persons she had ever known. We did not know there was a name for my problem and later learned it is called *dyslexia*.

Despite any problems, we felt confident we could start a family of our own. I was twenty-nine and she was twenty-four, and we agreed it was time. We were still living in our second apartment when, in January of 1970, our daughter, Jackie, was born. In this picture, Jackie is a couple of weeks old. She was so tiny and incredibly beautiful.

Al and daughter, Jackie

That was absolutely the most wonderful thing ever in my life. Having a baby brought my wife and me closer together. We did believe that someday we might have another child. Bonnie went back to work full time in 1974, and time passed so quickly. We just had one child, and she was great. We left it at that.

During the first few years of Jackie's life, Bonnie would read books to her. There were times that I wished so much that I could also read to my daughter, but that was not possible. Sometimes I pretended to read from a book. I just made up a story. My daughter enjoyed it and didn't know the difference.

When she was a baby, our reading levels were the same. This really deepened my feelings of inadequacy, and I felt helpless to change anything. So I just went along.

When Jackie was a little older, it was a very different story; she could read. There were times when she asked me to read something. I always had a reason why I was not able to read just then, like "I don't have my glasses on" or "I'll catch you later" or "Ask your mother." My daughter didn't know I could not read until she was an adult.

Jackie had been born in January 1970 and was as normal as normal can be. Bonnie stopped working to stay home with her for the first four and half years. Money was really tight, but we felt Jackie would benefit from being home with Mom for the early years.

In retrospect, we were right. Jackie spent three weeks in kindergarten and was passed through to first grade because the teacher felt that kindergarten held no challenge for her. Bonnie attended parent/teacher conferences. But after a while, there was nothing they could offer to improve the learning and comprehension abilities of our daughter. She graduated as valedictorian from her high school in 1987, attended college, became a professor, and now has her doctorate. She teaches her students (our future teachers) methods for teaching mathematics to elementary, middle, and high school students.

All in all, there were good times, and there were bad times. I felt my bad times were all in the past, and I was pretty happy. I had a job, a home, a wife, and a daughter. I felt sure I could accomplish anything I wanted.

Bonnie took care of paying the bills and keeping us on track. I knew that if there were any problems, we could certainly handle them together. As far as reading went, I can't recall a time when my not being able to read was an issue. Bonnie was always there when it mattered.

In 1969 Bonnie had stopped working when she became pregnant. In 1974, she went back to work full time. This made me very happy. It meant more income, and more freedom. I felt pretty cool with myself. For the past few years, my usual pattern had been to go out with the boys every Friday night—and I mean *every* Friday night. After a couple of years of this, I know my wife was getting very tired of the routine and, in fact, worried. She usually waited up for me and usually was very pleasant when I got home. The evenings when I returned at two or three in the morning, things were not as cheerful. Yes, I did have a lot of fun, and although I knew Bonnie was not happy about this routine, well, that's the way it was.

So we went on. I felt I was basically a good and caring person. And I know my wife thought so too. I've made mistakes. Haven't we all? Eventually, things (I mean I) simmered down a bit. I thought maybe my friends changed, or maybe I changed. But somehow I felt going out every week was getting a little tiring or, realistically speaking, boring. I started to realize that strutting my stuff was really not where it's at.

Life catches up with us all sooner or later, and we begin to realize what is important to us. After many years, I realized that going out drinking and partying "with the boys" was not all that it was cracked up to be. Coming home to a loving family is where it's at, entirely. Just maybe, my own family, which, by the way, we both chose to create, was what mattered most.

Now I go out (usually) every Monday night and meet with a group of cool guys from my Corvette Club. In fact, my wife not only encourages me to go out, she asks me to go. She believes that married couples need to have their own space every once in a while. I agree. We meet at a restaurant and just talk and have a great time.

Bonnie and I have belonged to the Chicago Corvette Club since 2013. It is a large organization, started in 1958, and we have many new good friends because of it. So many years ago, I could not have imagined owning my own Corvette. Among many other cars, I've owned a Buick Wildcat, a Riviera, a GTO, and a Mustang—very fast cars. But the Corvette; the best ever!

CHAPTER 10
Service

When I was around fifteen years old, two of my oldest brothers, Leroy and Carl, joined the US Armed Forces.

Dad used to hit Carl a lot. Carl was forced to sit next to him at the dinner table so just in case he got out of line, my dad would whack him. My dad said Carl was always up to no good. I'm not sure what went on between my dad and my brother Leroy, but I think both Leroy and Carl enlisted to get away from home.

When I was about twenty-five years old, I got a letter in the mail from the US government. It was from the draft board, and I was ordered to go in to sign up. First I had to have a physical exam, which I passed. Then I went into a big room and was given a rather large form to fill out. I was nervous and afraid I may be drafted into the army.

One form was math problems and was about twenty pages long. I tried my best to answer the problems. Some of the questions required reading, so I just passed them by. I think I might have gotten a few right. The other form had all to do with reading. I really tried, for many hours, but I knew I was not going to get through the form at all.

After three or four hours, my time was up, and I had to turn in my papers. I don't recall if someone talked to me that day or a few days later. They might have suspected that I was purposely pretending I could not read and probably checked into my school records to verify whether or not I could read. Soon thereafter, I received a notice in the mail that I was denied admission and was classified as 4F: not qualified for military service. I was sad—and I was very happy.

I never told anyone of my unsatisfactory classification, only that I was not called for duty because I was married. My brother-in-law, who was the same age as me, was also married. How odd, I told my friends, that he got drafted and not me.

CHAPTER 11
Illinois Tool Works

After Bonnie and I were married, I found a new job near our apartment in Chicago at Illinois Tool Works (ITW). My life was changing. As expected, the usual problem came up at the interview: they asked me to fill out the application which, of course, I couldn't. I said I didn't have time right then to do it, and I asked if I could take the application home and bring it back the next day. They agreed. Great! Bonnie and I filled it out. The next day, I returned with the filled-out application.

We talked for a while about my experience in operating lathes and milling machines. They showed me around the plant. I was hired. On my first day, the machine I was to start working on was a lathe, and I was shown how to operate it. I picked up on it pretty well. There were many challenges, but I had a new job that paid more money.

For the next year, I was operating two to four different lathes and milling machines. But it was getting boring. I needed a job with more of a challenge and that paid more money. I started talking to coworkers, asking if they knew of other jobs that would pay more and be more interesting.

These are pictures from an ITW Open House in 1974. The first picture is of Joe, who has been my friend for many years. The second is a picture of me with my wife, Bonnie, and our daughter, Jackie, standing between us. She was just four years old. My brother Norman was there also.

Al's friend Joe

Bonnie, Norman, Jackie, Al

My title was machine operator. I made metal cutting tools used to make gears and other mechanical components. I got to know some guys in the precision grinding department. That work had to be very precise, and it paid more. Thanks to connections with one of the bosses I had made friends with, I got into that department.

My title now was precision hob grinder. With verbal help from others, I got pretty good at it. Metal pieces were processed in stages. I would get a piece from the back-off department, and my job was to fine-tune it into a sharp precision cutting tool. They were used to cut metal into gears for the automotive industries and other applications. Sometimes my piece came back from the final inspection department for correction.

Part of my job was becoming computerized; they now wanted me to run a computer in order to run the machine. Wow! I had to copy the instructions and take them home so Bonnie and I could decipher what they meant. I'd go back the next day and try to apply this to operating my machine. These times were very tense and very stressful.

I got to know more people at work, and I made it a point to talk to them in order to better understand the operation of my machinery. I asked about a job in another department where I could possibly make more money. I realized that in order to make more money, I would have to make friends with the higher-ups, like the supervisors and administrative personnel, hoping they would put in a good word for me. It is a very big company, and there were more people to know and more money to make—all without fussing with this reading business.

Occasionally I was asked to read something, but I always had an excuse for not reading it and found a way around the problem. For instance, one time the boss asked me to read a chart. I said I didn't want to read it. Then I just turned around and walked out. I was so surprised I got away with that.

Back at my job in mid-1980, when I was confronted with using a computer in connection with operating machinery, my supervisor asked me to write down the instructions as he read them to me. Sure, like there was any remote possibility of that happening? There were a few times I said, "I'd get to that right away" (and take it home with me), and a few times I asked my instructor if he wouldn't mind writing it down for me, saying I was such a terrible speller. Unbelievably, it worked. He wrote the instructions down, and I later took them home.

This game I had to play was getting very tiresome. I was just very lucky I was able to take papers home. No one questioned what I was doing. I would just change the subject or create some other distraction. A coworker of mine had a little difficulty in reading the instructions, but it seemed he had more difficulty in understanding what he had read. I believe I was able to help him get through it by showing him what I had learned.

Fifteen years had gone by, and I was getting comfortable with my job. They approached me with an invitation to be part of the public relations group to welcome out-of-state gear school participants. This was a fun job. It was all talking, eating, drinking, and socializing while we discussed operating machinery and various aspects of the role ITW had in this vast industry. I felt I made these people feel comfortable, and I was making a real contribution for my employer.

Times were good. My health was good. My home life with my wife and daughter was going along very well. Bonnie and I enjoyed socializing with family and friends. But that computer thing kept creeping into my job world. I was approached a couple of times by the bosses, asking if I would be interested in a position in management instead of operating machinery. I said I would think about it. But I knew that position involved writing and reading reports, and other situations I surely could not handle or take home with me. I had to turn down the promotions.

I was now fifty-four years old, and I was just going along, doing the same old thing every day. The job was very repetitious—actually, monotonous. Of course, it's surprise time. Someone threw a monkey wrench into the machinery (not literally). I was informed that my company was doing a cutback in our department and I could continue doing the same job if I transferred to their plant in Rockford, Illinois. I'm thinking, *Hmm, Rockford. That's near where I was born back in 1940. How ironic is that!* It seemed like I was going back in time, and I felt that I had no other choice but to resign.

I was out of a job for about one month. I talked with a few of my friends who happened to be supervisors of a division of ITW. (Connections are so important.) I was able to be interviewed and was offered a position in the screw-making department. It was a big machine, lots of oil, lots of noise. But it was a job. It took me three to four months to really get a handle on operating that machine.

That position continued for about a year, and I decided it was my time to retire. I was offered a good retirement package, and after twenty-nine years, it was time to go down a different road.

CHAPTER 12
Vacations

After our glorious vacation (honeymoon) in Milwaukee in July of 1964, we went various places now and then. Our first big trip was driving to Miami, Florida, in the summer of 1967. We had a Buick Wildcat, and most of the time we were cruising along at about ninety miles an hour. Our first stop was Chattanooga, Tennessee. We had packed a lunch and ate along the way so we didn't have to stop often. There must have been something wrong with our food, because we both felt sick. We were back on the road in the morning and drove straight through to Miami.

It was a good time. I didn't have to worry about reading anything, because my wife was with me. The first day of our stay, we decided to go on a fishing boat. It was a charter boat, and I said I wanted to catch sailfish. We came upon a school of dolphin fish and started to bring in a few. My wife didn't want to fish, so the boat owner said she could just hold the pole, and he would do the rest. Her line got tangled in the motor behind the boat, and he was able to untangle it. But she was fired from the fishing job.

I wanted to stay out a little longer, so we were on that boat for five hours. I can't to this day believe we would have ever planned on staying on a boat that length of time with no hats, no shade, and no suntan lotion.

That evening my wife was in so much pain, it was awful. Her skin was dark red. She put some product on her skin that was supposed to give you an artificial tan and woke up the next morning with what looked like a beautiful tan. I didn't burn as bad as she did. Eventually, her skin blistered and peeled. Great time again.

We didn't realize it, but we had chosen to go to Florida during hurricane season. We were nearly blown down by the velocity of the wind, and the undertow of the ocean kept us from going in the water. But, all in all, it was a very nice trip. We met a nice couple, went to dinners and shows, and survived the vacation.

In 1974, we started going on vacation with my wife's sister, Kathy, and her husband, Bert. Our daughter was four years old then. We had great times in the Lake of the Ozarks in Missouri and did that for the next four or five years. They had an eighteen-foot motorboat, and we had a great time water skiing and just cruising around. Again, there was no issue with my lack of reading abilities. They were not aware I had a problem, nor was there a reason I felt they needed to know. It was absolutely amazing I was able to disguise my secret.

At age thirty, I went skiing in Aspen, Colorado, with five guys, including my brother-in-law, Bert. It was the first vacation that I didn't have my wife along to help. One evening I got lost trying to find the street for the resort. This place was completely new to me, and none of the letters on the street signs looked familiar. I walked around for quite a while until I knew where I was. The guys asked me what took me so long to get back, and I used the excuse that I went shopping.

After that, I stayed with my brother-in-law most of the time so I wouldn't get lost. He didn't know I had a reading problem; none of them did. We all had a great time skiing. However, we had to label our luggage with our home addresses in case it got lost. One of the guys asked me to put his name and address on his luggage. I knew his address, but I didn't know how to spell either his name or his address, so I pulled out my address from my wallet and put that on his luggage. I was very worried he would notice, but he never did. I had gotten by again.

CHAPTER 13
College of DuPage

Jackie went on to college and majored in the teaching of mathematics. One day when she was home on break, she was in our kitchen with me, and I asked her to read the next step written on the box of the food I was preparing for dinner. She was busy, so she said, "No, you read it." I made some excuses and asked her again. She said, "Sorry, I can't right now. You read it." After a long pause, I simply said, "I can't.

The cat was out of the bag. She didn't understand why I had kept it a secret all those years. Then she realized why I had never read her a story from a book. I usually made up the story, but I couldn't keep that up. She now understood why it was always Mom's place to help with her homework. She had probably thought that's what moms do.

Enter Jackie

Jackie found out that the College of DuPage (COD) had a program for adult illiteracy and suggested I enroll in a course. I was then fifty-five and had taken an early retirement at ITW. I tried reading to show her how my reading was—actually, was *not*. I was not able to get 98 percent of the words correct.

She and I went to COD to get information and fill out the forms to start with an adult illiteracy program. They said I would have to take a test to find my placement in a reading class. Jackie explained I was not able to take a test because I couldn't read. They persisted. She also persisted and said, "If you force my dad to take this test, he will just walk out and never come back." They waived the test, and I later started classes.

Our teacher, Renai Graham, used a curriculum called the Wilson Reading System, which used a multisensory approach. The program now is known as Wilson Language Training. She showed us videos of people's mouths to show what our mouth looks like when we annunciate words. We talked about the alphabet and phonics. We even had a discussion on the beginning of the creation of letters and what sounds they had from the beginning of recorded time. She was giving us the key to unlock words.

Her classes were small, and I felt very comfortable and unthreatened. No one in our class laughed or criticized others for their inability to read. She really inspired confidence in her students.

We would take a single letter and tap our fingers as we were sounding out the letters. We also would go over the short and long sounds of letters. Renai used flash cards and tapes. We all took turns reading. No one made fun of anyone for mispronouncing a word or going too slow. That was great. We were all trying to get to the same place.

Renai also dictated a sentence, and we had to write it. The class was very challenging. She explained that the sense of touch is connected to the right side of the brain, which may be a strength of some learning disabled people.

At first, the classes were basic beginning reading with words no longer than three letters. More importantly, I was introduced to phonics in a different way. We would tap out the sounds with our fingers as we spoke the sound of a letter. She explained that the tapping prevents readers from dropping or adding sounds, a characteristic of dyslexia. Each sound needs one tap.

It was hard work and kind of frustrating doing that at my age. But everyone there was trying just as hard as I was.

Everyone was kind and respectful to each other. This was not like the classes in schools that I was used to in Chicago so many years earlier.

Now someone was actually helping me to sound out letters. Book 1 was very difficult. We worked on that book for what seemed to be a very long time. I felt that I was doing pretty well until I got my first test results. I failed, and my hopes of reading suddenly went out the window. *What now?* I wondered.

When I talked to my teacher about my failure, she said not to be too disappointed, because most students had trouble with book 1. She added that repeating the course would make a big difference. She was right. I studied even harder, and finally I passed the test. Book 2 was basically a continuation of book 1, but once in a while we had words with four letters.

The English language is so difficult, mainly because of the exceptions to the rules. There are so many exceptions, and there are also so many rules!

My friend Frank and I worked together quite often, and we both felt we were really making headway at about the time we progressed to book 3. We were to accomplish getting through book 12 before graduating. Books 6 and 7 were very advanced, as now we were working with four- to five-syllable words, but we kept going. We had to break up each word by syllables. It helped to know that every syllable must have a vowel. That was a good rule. The real difficulty begins when there are exceptions to the rules.

With Renai's help, we were able to work on computers. We would practice typing words and changing their forms, like present tense, past tense, and many other lessons.

I went on to take the test for my GED high school equivalency diploma. It was extremely difficult, and I didn't pass, but I still make an effort to read. After five years in this class, my friend Frank and I were to take the Illinois State Test for adult literacy. Because of our difficulty with reading, there was no time limit on our test. We were in the same room, and we sat a great distance from one another. I don't know if it was because we studied together for so many years or what, but we both got the exact same items right and the exact same items wrong. They accused us of cheating, but there was absolutely no cheating.

Frank and I attended the College of DuPage for eight years. I had passed the tests, and I got a diploma of completion. When the State of Illinois canceled this adult illiteracy class, I was done with classes. But Frank continued taking a similar class, which he had to pay for. The previous classes we took for all those years had been totally funded by the State of Illinois.

At the College of DuPage, our teacher would give us a few words and asked us to make a sentence out of each word. That was hard, but I did it. After a while, it got a little easier, because we were allowed to use a Franklin speller in class. We would put the word in the machine, and it would say the word and give us the definition. That was great, because if I didn't know what a word was, the machine would simply tell me. I wouldn't be as frustrated when I couldn't read one word in a sentence.

After five or six years, I felt very good about my new ability to read. My reading level, which had started out at zero grade level, according to Renai, was now at a grade level of 5.5. That was good, and I was happy. I could now read most signs, and I could pick out cards for birthdays, graduations, anniversaries, etc., and actually read the messages. I got rather good at that.

When I went back to school at age fifty-five, I never felt so good. I wish I could always feel that good. I walked in the classroom and walked down the halls, looking at students and teachers, and I knew we were all there for one reason: education. I had my homework in my bag as I strutted through the halls.

It's hard to put it into words, but I felt great! It was like I really belonged there, and I was proud. I was a little older than some of the students, but I didn't care. I just felt good. I sat down in a classroom with people just like me, who were talking to me like normal.

After a week or two of school, I started to put words together. I could have never done that before. After a while, I was saying the ABCs every day and night and on weekends to improve. When saying the ABCs, I also said the sound that each letter made. I was learning the alphabet and the sounds of each letter quite well.

I practiced different letter combinations to put words together. After about one year, I felt I was finally getting a better understanding of the structure of words, and it was becoming a little easier. Spelling was even harder. There are so many combinations!

What really felt good about going back to school was that I met a lot of new friends. I never realized there were so many people with problems like me. After about two years, when a new person came to the class, my teacher would ask me to work with that person one on one to see where he or she was at when it came to reading. I could really see that I wasn't alone when it came to having a reading problem. The people in my class probably had good jobs working in schools, offices, and factories, but they were struggling just like me.

In our class, we all sat there taking turns reading to each other. I felt very comfortable with them. We all had one common goal, and that made me feel good.

Frank and I became good friends. We met one hour before class started twice a week so we could study together. We would talk and talk about words, letters, and sounds and would read out loud to each other before we had class. He was a nice guy. We continued studying together for many years. I have to admit that he spelled a little better than me, but that's okay.

I achieved a great deal in school, met new friends, and had a wonderful teacher. She helped everybody. So after eight years, I completed the course and felt I was better equipped to handle basic reading and spelling.

Today, as I'm writing this book, I know I'll never be a real great reader, but I achieved more than I imagined. The English language is very hard, but I did my best.

When I got out of school, I worked part time at the civil engineering firm in Rosemont, where my wife was also employed. She worked there for twenty-four years and retired in 2010. I worked there for five years. Among many other responsibilities, some of my duties included alphabetical filing and retrieving documents from the archives—unbelievably—and doing errands with company cars, which sometimes involved reading maps. I found it much easier to read instructions, menus, streets names, and signs. It felt like a new world. I never felt so good driving my car and being able to read street signs.

I had a very neat trick I used to get around. I would carry a little handheld recorder and record information. If someone was giving me an address over the phone, I would listen, repeat what I heard, and not have to worry about writing it down. It usually worked, and they didn't know I was recording their voice. I was pretty happy I discovered this tool.

The hardest part was telling all my friends I had finally learned to read. I've known some of them for over fifty years. One very good friend, Joe, said I should have told him sooner, because he could have helped me get a better job. What always held me back was thinking people would think I was not very intelligent. So I had to keep up this front for my own protection. I enjoyed talking to people, and I felt they respected me for who I am.

I know people like me who deal with dyslexia have many good qualities. We are intelligent and unique in our own way; we just have to give an extra effort, be kind and compassionate, and get along with people. Others may take their easily learned ability to read for granted, but those like me believe that learning how to read is one of the greatest accomplishments ever.

I am proud to say that, after going to the College of DuPage, I decided it was time for me to be in charge of writing all checks and balancing both checking and savings accounts at home. This, in itself, has given me a renewed sense of pride in my abilities. Once in a while, I get frustrated when, after many tries, I can't balance the checking account. That's when I hand it over to Bonnie, and she finds the problem every time. I also like to cook and my wife loves it. What more can I say?

CHAPTER 14
Reading Program

When I went back to school at the College of DuPage, my first book was from the Barbara Wilson Program, book 1. My teacher said I had to memorize all the concepts of sounds in order to read. It was a challenge because all I see is a bunch of letters. As I was taught, words are made up of sounds, so if I wanted to read, I had to learn all the different blends of sounds. Take for instance, the *th* sound, as in *thumb*. Your tongue has to come out slightly. So my teacher told us to bring a mirror to the classroom. She told us to look at our tongue in our mirror when we talked. I had never given any thought before to see how I formed my words.

From the very beginning, one of our books was a workbook, which had various exercises in it. The problem was that you had to read the instructions at the top, telling you what to do. However, not too many of us were able to read those instructions, so our teacher had to read them for us for a while. She would say some letters and slowly sound out the sounds until we all were picking it up.

Book 1 was very hard, and I flunked. There were twelve books. Although I failed book 1, my teacher said it was okay. She told me that when I did it again, I would pass. And I did. I went on to book 2 and never felt so good, because I found it to be easier.

I never imagined our language was so complicated. There are many sounds in the English language consisting of long and short vowels, consonants, diphthongs, silent letters, the R-control factor, and so much more. Wow!

Each day it felt like a miracle that I was putting letters together and making basic words. They were small words, but I was able to put them into sentences. It was a challenge, and I had never thought that this accomplishment would make me feel this good. I had been going to the College of DuPage (COD) for a little over a year, and every day was fun. I was grateful that, now that I was retired, I had the time and energy to attend school regularly.

I had to work really hard, because all vowels are difficult in that they each have three distinct sounds. Take for example the letter A. A word with a long vowel is **a**ble, a short vowel is **at**, and a schwa or slurred vowel is **a**nother. Wow! This was all Greek to me.

The teacher would give us a list of what they refer to as consonant blends, such as CR, SL, and TR etc. The sounds were at both the beginning and the ends of words. They were difficult sounds, and I found them hard to learn, but every day it seemed to get a little easier.

I would come home after school and practice the sounds of each letter in the alphabet. I would record my voice saying a sentence and then slowly write it down as I pronounced each word. It gave me more time to understand each word. I found it difficult sometimes, but eventually it got a little easier.

By the time I progressed to books 5 and 6, I noticed there were different combinations of letters in some words that didn't follow the usual pattern. I asked the teacher why this different combination was acceptable, and she said, "It is an exception to the rule." I found that there were many exceptions to the rule. I guess that's the English language for you.

There were times in the classroom that I had to read from a book in front of the other students. At first, it was a little hard, but it did get easier with time. The other students also read in front of the class, so no one was embarrassed. We were all reading together. Some students read a little better than others, but we were all pushing through.

When we got to book 7, the words got longer and more difficult. We were now dealing with words containing four to seven syllables. Our teacher instructed us to take one syllable at a time and slowly get through the word. For example, I would look at a six-syllable word like *excommunication* and see ex-com-mu-ni-ca-tion. At that point I had spoken (read) the word, and it was the most wonderful feeling.

Speaking at the Barbara Wilson program teacher conference:

Now that I was retired at age fifty-five and I had been enrolled in an adult literacy class at the College of DuPage for about three years, my teacher, Renai Graham, said there was an English reading teacher conference coming up that would focus on the Wilson teaching system. She wanted me to attend the meeting and asked me if I could speak to the teachers on behalf of the program, explaining how the method was working for me. I was expected to talk, not read, so of course, I said yes.

The teacher conference was held at a hotel in downtown Chicago. It was all very exciting to be part of it. I was sitting in the back of the room with Renai. Then Barbara Wilson asked me to come up to the podium and explain how her program had benefited me.

At first, when I looked around the room and saw some eighty or ninety teachers that would be teaching the Wilson program, I was nervous. They asked me what I thought was the hardest part of learning the alphabet. I replied that I had trouble with nonsense words; these were one-syllable, made-up words that I had to sound out. For example, a nonsense word could be *clem* or *jumb,* and we would have to figure out how this made-up word would sound. After you successfully say the word, you do not recognize it, because it's not a word and has no meaning. But when you're told you did pronounce it correctly, you feel you've accomplished something important.

When I think back about that now, I realize that, to me, all words were nonsense until my good teacher spent quality time with me. This system really helped me to analyze letter sounds that made up words. I was overwhelmed with the importance of this meeting, and I was so honored to be a part of it.

I thought I was a pretty smart guy because I could say four- and five-syllable words. When using this system in our class, we tapped our fingers with each syllable. This helped us to recognize all the correct sounds within the word.

A few teachers in the conference asked me questions. One asked what my reading grade level was. I told them that when I started back in 1995, my reading grade level was zero. By the year 1998, my reading level was at 4.1. I was pretty happy about that.

Teachers are amazing! And I do believe that program helped me all around to read the real words better. This program works quite well, but it took me a lot of time and effort, probably because of my age.

Renai told me she was proud of me when I spoke to all those teachers. That made her feel good, and it made me feel even better. Learning to read has made me stronger and more positive in everything I do. I found it very exciting talking to those teachers, and I now feel confident I can talk to anyone on any level and be comfortable.

CHAPTER 15
National TV

Things were looking up. I was retired and feeling more comfortable with the fact that I was able to read far better than I had ever imagined in my life. I could now relax a little, not having to go to work and being challenged by words, and having feelings of inadequacy because of my problem. I was just a regular everyday person.

At that point in my life, I was now free to tell people that I had a reading problem and was not ashamed to admit it. In fact, with all the help I'd finally gotten from teachers, I was quite proud of my accomplishments. It really was a huge weight off my shoulders when I realized I did not have to hide my secret anymore.

Enter my daughter, Jackie, to the rescue again. She had a brilliant idea. She jokingly said, "Now that you've told everyone your news, maybe I could write a letter to Oprah Winfrey and tell her, too!" We'd heard that the famous talk show celebrity was proposing to do a show to feature a chosen group of individuals who were trying to overcome a personal problem and tell the viewing audience what their goal was for the upcoming millennium. So I said, "Sure." Jackie wrote the following letter, dated December 29, 1997, to the producers of *The Oprah Winfrey Show.*

Jackie Murawska
2917 N. Halsted Apt. G
Chicago, IL 60657

December 29, 1997

Oprah Show
ATTN: Show Ideas
P.O. Box 909715
Chicago, IL 60690

Dear Oprah and Producers:

I have an idea for show: adult literacy. Even if you've explored this topic before, perhaps you would consider highlighting it again because of its importance.

The reason I am writing now is because my father, now 57 years old and retired, has been illiterate throughout his adult life. You would never have guessed he couldn't read...because he is the life of any party, a great conversationalist, and obviously an intelligent man! In fact, I did not find out until I was a sophomore in college (when my dad has asked me to read directions for him from a microwave dinner box). The only other people who knew his secret were my mother and his mother. For the rest of his family and friends, he used many clever excuses to hide his problem—e.g. doesn't have his glasses today, too tired to read or write, etc.

My dad, Al, had to compensate in different ways in order to keep his job as a precision grinder, to find his way while driving in the city or on expressways, or to choose an entree off of a menu. (I believe he knew how to recognize many key words even though he wasn't able to sound them out using phonics.) Of course, my mother, Bonnie, has helped immensely on countless occasions through the years by filling out forms, preparing taxes and paying bills, in addition to trying to give my father reading and phonics lessons. I, too, wanted to help so I became a literacy volunteer to learn how to teach basic reading while pursuing my undergraduate degree in math education. When home from college, I worked with my father on pronunciation and basic reading skills...but once a month lessons didn't help—he needed a class which met more regularly.

The good news is that one year ago, my father enrolled in an adult basic education class at the College of DuPage. He was reluctant at first, as he thought the other students would be "dumb," or that the majority would be non-English speaking students; however, he found that the others were just like him. With the guidance of a wonderful teacher, he began in book "0" and within one year, he has already advanced to reading at a 4.5 grade level. Needless to say, a whole world has opened up for my dad. When driving down the street, he often reads signs along the way. When watching television, he reads any words on the screen. At Christmas gatherings, he can write his own grab bag wish list. (I could go on and on!) He does his homework religiously. Soon he will write a check for the first time.

We are so proud of him! It took a lot of courage to go back to school after not having been to school since the age of 14. When talking with him about his class and schoolwork, he too beams with pride; it's been a long road filled with a lot of hard work.

A couple of weeks ago, the Chicago Tribune did an article about this topic and interviewed students in my father's class and took photographs. My dad opted to have them take a picture of his face (most students were too embarrassed and requested only "back of the head" or close-up "hand" shots). They did indeed print his picture, and a number of things about my dad! (See enclosed article.) As you can see, one reason why my dad had trouble learning to read in the past was because he just now found out he has dyslexia.

Now that the article and picture has come out, my father decided to tell everyone the secret he has been keeping all these years. He told his best friend, his brothers and sisters, in-laws and neighbors, and mailed copies of the newspaper article as well. Most everyone was completely surprised when they heard the news; they assumed everyone can read!

It seems like a huge burden has been lifted off his shoulders. And now that he has realized the joy (and importance) of reading, he wants to share his story to try to help other adults with reading difficulties or dyslexia by convincing them to take a class and start learning to read.

Again, my family and I couldn't be more proud of my father. I hope you consider calling him or myself to find out more details, as there are so many. Before this letter is sent, my dad will have read it, so he will be aware of everything I have written about him.

Thank you very much for your time.

Sincerely,

Jackie Murawska

Jackie Murawska

Home:
Jackie Murawska
2917 N. Halsted Apt. G
Chicago, IL 60657
773-388-1217
    best times to call: evenings

Letter to Oprah from Jackie

We waited for a response, and to our astonishment, a producer called and invited my daughter and me to be guests on the show. For the first show (there were three), my daughter and I were picked up in a limo and brought to the studio green room for hair and makeup. There was a small group of other people there to also talk about their individual goals for the millennium. It was a very exciting, busy place. I was surprised there was no rehearsal before going on national television, in front of a live audience.

I talked about my journey so far and my struggles to just get by. My goal for the millennium was "I want to read." As I remember it, during my interview by the producer, I was asked which book I would choose to read from. Having seen and enjoyed the movie, I decided on *To Kill a Mockingbird* by Harper Lee. Oprah gave that book to me and asked if I would read from it. I answered, "Yes, I guarantee it." It was fantastic, and one of the biggest highlights of my life!

In preparation for my second appearance on the show, a TV crew came to my home to film and record me as I was being interviewed about my reading goals. They also filmed and talked with Bonnie in our living room.

The crew followed me to the College of DuPage, filming me walking down the halls and into my classroom, where I sat with my fellow students and my teacher, Renai. This was one of the most profound experiences that had ever happened to me. It was an honor and privilege to be part of that television program.

On my third and final appearance, I was allowed to invite some of my other family members. My wife and daughter also attended the taping and sat right in the front row. They said the experience was overwhelming. For that final show, we were all picked up and returned to our homes in limousines. I felt like a celebrity.

During the last show, it was time to actually read a section from *To Kill a Mockingbird*. Coincidently, Oprah said that was one of her favorite books. I had seen the motion picture with Gregory Peck, and I picked a section where he was talking in the courtroom. I chose that section because it had a very strong message. Oprah sat right next to me while I read.

I'd like to reprint that particular portion here, which I introduced as follows: "I would like to read a segment of the book *To Kill a Mockingbird*, which takes place in the courtroom where Atticus is addressing the jury."

We know all men are not created equal in the sense some people would have us believe— some people are smarter than others, some people have more opportunity because they're born with it, some men make more money than others, some ladies make better cakes than others—some people are born gifted beyond the normal scope of most men.

But there is one way in this country in which all men are created equal—there is one human institution that makes a pauper the equal of a Rockefeller, the stupid man the equal of an Einstein, and the ignorant man the equal of any college president. That institution, gentlemen, is a court. It can be the Supreme Court of the United States or the humblest J.P. court in the land, or this honorable court which you serve. Our courts have their faults, as does any human institution, but in this country our courts are the great levelers, and in our courts all men are created equal. (Lee 1960, 12.)

Someone told me that this book was at a twelfth-grade reading level because of the slang. At that time, I was reading at a 5.5 grade level. I had to practice a lot. It was very tense. I know both my wife and daughter were sitting on the edge of their seats, listening to me. I got through it and felt on top of the world.

Talk about boosting one's confidence! All those moments revolving around that experience will remain forever embedded in my heart and soul.

Jackie, I really made it, thanks to your loving help. My extreme appreciation goes out to the gracious hostess of the show, Oprah, for letting me be a part of the program. I hope that your allowing me to "come out" and admit on national TV that I had a problem and wanted to do something about it, may have helped others. I thank you so much.

When I was on that show, my voice was very hoarse. I didn't know it at the time, but I had throat cancer. Later, the cancer was successfully removed. However, a few years later, I had another surgery to remove more cancer, with two surgeons operating on me. One removed a kidney and the other removed a portion of my colon. Miraculously, no chemo or radiation was necessary. I got past that one, too. Someone must be watching over me.

CHAPTER 16
Publications

Following is a copy of a page from the 1998 issue of *The Decoder,* which is published semiannually by Wilson Language Training out of Massachusetts; it's a brief article about my appearance on *The Oprah Winfrey Show.* I was so honored.

Barbara and Ed Wilson

BULK RATE
US POSTAGE
PAID
HOLLISTON, MA
PERMIT NO. 72

Address Service Requested

READING
SYSTEM

Wilson on prime time with Oprah and Al Lewis!

Al Lewis, age 57, prepares to place a Step 4 Wilson workbook into a Year 2000 Chest on the Oprah Winfrey Show. Al is finally learning to read with his Wilson teacher, Renee Graham. He can already do some things he has always wanted to do such as read labels at the grocery store and select food from menus. He is especially proud of reading aloud to his brother. He told Oprah Winfrey that his goal is to read the book, *To Kill a Mockingbird* by the year 2000. There is no doubt, he will. He expressed complete confidence when he said to Oprah that he will do it, "guaranteed."

Article in *The Decoder* regarding Al
on *The Oprah Winfrey Show*

Just one more letter of recognition I would like to proudly present was from the Secretary of State Literacy Office/Illinois State Library. With their permission, following is a copy of the letter to me, dated April 25, 2000, from the Literacy Program Director, Judith A. Rake.

OFFICE OF THE SECRETARY OF STATE

JESSE WHITE • Secretary of State

SECRETARY OF STATE LITERACY OFFICE/ILLINOIS STATE LIBRARY
431 S. Fourth
Springfield, Illinois 62701
217/785-6921

April 25, 2000

Mr. Alby "Al" Lewis
368 Golfview
Bloomingdale, IL 60108

Dear Mr. Lewis:

    Secretary of State Jesse White, David Bennett of the Illinois Press Association and all of us involved in the Illinois literacy effort would like to express our admiration for your accomplishments in adult learning. We can understand why you are one of your literacy program's outstanding students.

    Although you were not selected to receive the Spotlight on Achievement Award, the fact that you were nominated from more than 29,000 adult students truly makes your accomplishments remarkable. In the very near future, you will be receiving a certificate of recognition as a participant in the Spotlight on Achievement Award program.

    Providing literacy classes and dedicated tutors for all interested students is a priority for Secretary White, and you have the support of this office in your further pursuit of learning. You should be very proud of all you have achieved.

Sincerely,

Judith A. Rake
Literacy Program Director

JAR:dm
cc: Ruta Jonusaitis, College of DuPage

Springfield, Illinois 62756

Letter from the Illinois Secretary of State

I believe it doesn't matter where you are from; it matters where you are going. From my humble beginning to the present day, I am fortunate to have had the help and encouragement of so many people. I do not want to appear to be bragging, but I believe reading disorders can be overcome by all those who seek help.

CHAPTER 17
North Central College

At my daughter's place of employment, North Central College (NCC), I was invited several times to speak to classes of future teachers of elementary, middle school, and high school students.

I would begin by telling the students about myself and some of the obstacles I faced while growing up with an inability to read or write, and how I coped with it. I explained there were three segments in my life:

First, I was born into an extremely poor family. The school system in Chicago apparently was not equipped to recognize reading problems in children. It seemed they could not distinguish between behavioral issues and a genuine inability to read.

Second, joining the workforce was an extreme challenge. I could not even fill out job applications or any other forms that required even the least amount of reading. Those were obstacles I had to overcome. Getting my driver's license and reading street signs was another big issue.

And finally, with the welcomed and persistent help of my daughter and my wife, I challenged myself, pushed aside my self-consciousness, and went back to school.

That part of my talk would usually take about half an hour. In the discussions that followed, the students would ask questions about my past and present challenges. Jackie brought up a very good thought: there are more issues than what meets the eye when dealing with young children. So much depends on the child's family and social life. A child in a very poor family might not have eaten in a day or two. Some children come from broken homes or have abusive parents. It is hard to concentrate on lessons in school when you are hungry or tired or sick. Teachers should keep that in mind when a child is having difficulty and try to find out what is going on.

I have been asked on several occasions to speak at my daughter's college, and I consider it a great honor. If I can help a teacher understand how it was from a child's perspective, I feel I have done a great service.

My wife was at most of these meetings, and she was asked about how she felt living with me and my problem. She had suspected I had an issue with reading early in our relationship. We talked about it, and to her, it was not an issue. She told the class in one of the meetings, "Al's reading ability was not what attracted me to him."

Bonnie also recalled that when I was reading as she was looking on, I missed one word but kept on reading. To her amazement, the word I chose to substitute to keep the sentence flowing was a completely different word, but had the exact meaning as the one I could not read. This happened a few times, and she was perplexed. The word must have come through my brain by osmosis. I didn't understand it myself. Amazing!

We were again at North Central College (NCC) in March of 2014, speaking to a group of future teachers of middle school and high school students. My daughter and wife also have had questions for me and made comments at my speaking engagements at the college. Bonnie commented regarding the teachers I had in grade school, asking if it was possible that, because no one really knew what to do, they just pushed the problem (which was me) to the next class. Dyslexia was not a widely known disorder. It's possible that the teachers did not want to admit they had failed to teach a student to read.

Bonnie recalled that many years ago, she tried to help me by using the program "Hooked on Phonics." She and I got into the program many times, but it just wasn't working for me. She reminded me that I did not fail. She said she failed because she was not able to teach me. She was not a qualified teacher. Not until I went to the College of DuPage at age 55 did I have an excellent teacher, Renai Graham.

At all those speaking engagements at NCC, many of the teachers had comments to add during the sessions. During the March 2014 session, my wife noticed a teacher, Dr. Mary Beth Ressler, taking notes and later expressing her thoughts to the class. Impressed, Bonnie told Ms. Ressler she would like to incorporate that into my book. She sent her notes to me via email on March 5, 2014:

> It is important for our students to understand that reading abilities often have very little to do with a lack of intelligence. In fact, there were a variety of ways that Mr. Lewis demonstrated his intelligence in order to mask his difficulties with reading. Some of the strategies/coping mechanisms he used such as getting to know people—and the right people, memorizing important information such as area roads, navigating government systems (the DMV/

working the system by finding the right people to pay off), insulating himself by befriending bosses, using clever rhetorical maneuvers (when asked to read something—turning the statement back on the individual—"You read it. You are the boss"), copying text and utilizing [the help of] Mrs. Lewis to decode the text, all demonstrate this intelligence.

Because of my past struggles with learning how to read and having improved my abilities, I was fortunate to be a guest speaker several times at North Central College. The students there are future mathematics and English teachers of elementary, middle school, and high school students. I would talk about my firsthand experience as a person with a learning disability trying to grasp the English language.

I told them I was born in 1940, so back then, going to school in Chicago was not easy for me because I had dyslexia, which was not a well-known disorder back then. I said that new teachers need to understand the possible causes of a child having difficulty in the classroom. Some may have had no food since the day before, had no sleep, were in poor health, or lived in an abusive home. Some may have a sight or hearing problem or have dyslexia. Putting a child in the back of the classroom and pushing him or her through the system because the teachers think the child is lazy, a troublemaker, or just stupid is so very wrong. For so many years I felt that no one could help me understand why I had so much trouble with reading. I wondered what was wrong with me.

At first I was a little nervous talking to teachers, but as I progressed in my reading skills, I got more confident. I felt that if I could help even one child not just get through, but excel in school because I may have helped teachers be aware of potential problems and what to look for, I had helped in that effort.

During the course of my visits to North Central College, I received thank-you notes from some of the students—individual notes as well as group cards (about eighty students). It was overwhelming, to say the least. Most said they were impressed that I had taken the time to talk to them about my experiences as an illiterate student and impressed by my ability to survive through it all. Some said they admired my courage.

I was very moved by the comments these future teachers had after our discussions in their classroom. For example, they said I'd touched many lives by making them aware of my personal difficulties, and many said my messages would definitely affect their outlook when they became teachers.

They would make a special effort to be more aware of potential reading problems in their classrooms. I feel so honored to have reached out to these future teachers, and I thank each and every one of them for the experience of being with them.

CHAPTER 18
Grandchildren

My daughter, Jackie, was married in November of 1996 to her high school sweetheart, Jim. After a couple of years, they started a family. We were blessed with two beautiful grandchildren, Leah, born in 2000, and Ryan, born in 2002. I have had talks with them about the importance of paying attention at school and being truly interested in learning. They are fortunate they do not have a problem like mine.

When they were very young, I made a game of reciting the ABCs. We had three levels in our home, so as the kids and I were going up or down the stairs, we would say the individual sounds of each letter at each stair. They seemed to enjoy the game. This also reinforced my ability with the sounds of letters. They are both very active in sports and other activities and are remarkable children. We are so proud of them.

I can't believe it ever crossed my mind that any child (or grandchild) of mine would carry this unfortunate deficiency called dyslexia. My wife truly believed that something probably happened during my birth that caused my difficulty with the written word, and she didn't believe that a reading problem was contagious or hereditary. She considered me to be very intelligent.

I also can't imagine either one of my grandchildren—or any child—having the childhood I had. I can picture a little boy or girl at school being very frustrated because of the difficulty they find with reading and perhaps being teased by bullies. They struggle to be like the other children, but they know they are different. They get pushed around and many times get hurt. Like what happened to me, they are sent to the nurse's office, where she gives them a bandage and sends them home. The child goes home, and Mom looks at the wound, puts another bandage on her child, and says, "You're fine. Now go play." These are little children, and this is heartbreaking.

My daughter's school record was outstanding. At five years old, she spent two weeks in kindergarten before being sent to first grade. The teacher said kindergarten was not challenging enough for her. All through grade school, my wife went to her parent/teacher conferences. All of her teachers were impressed with Jackie's participation in and contributions to the class. She was an all-around good student and passed each grade with flying colors. The teachers and my wife were always able to have a nice chat about her.

Jackie continued to do equally as well in high school, and she was appointed valedictorian of the graduating class of 1987. She became a professor at age forty-three, and now she has earned her doctorate in mathematics education. She teaches math teachers how to teach mathematics to their students. We are beyond proud.

And now, from our daughter and her husband, Bonnie and I have two bright and happy grandchildren whose futures I'm sure will be very successful.

Leah is doing very well in school, and in 2014, while in seventh grade, she was inducted into the Junior National Honor Society. The three Rs did not seem to be difficult for her at all, and for me, the fact that she had no trouble reading was a giant relief.

Ryan seemed a little less interested in reading in first and second grades. That worried me. His teachers realized he might need some special help in that area and immediately had him put in a special reading class. I'm so glad my daughter also recognized there may be an issue and got right to it. Ryan is very self-confident and is getting almost straight A's.

Jackie, her husband, Jim, and children, Leah and Ryan

Both our grandchildren continue to be very involved in their school activities and continue to get good grades. To think that my daughter and grandchildren evolved as part of me; by the grace of God, I am so blessed.

CHAPTER 19
Thank You

A while ago I was striving for my GED. It seems like an eternity ago in my struggle to communicate using the written word. I finally feel I have reached a point in my life when I can relax and be thankful for a comfortable home, good health, and a loving family. I still have some difficulty with reading, but I no longer have feelings of inadequacy due to that shortcoming. I have learned a great deal along the way, and I feel I can read enough to get by. I do not belittle myself because of that anymore.

Like old times, my wife and I went horseback riding a couple of times. We don't roller-skate anymore—not since the last time in 2008, when Bonnie broke her left ankle at the roller rink.

We have enjoyed many activities since we joined the Chicago Corvette Club in 2013. We've made many new friends. Four of our good friends moved out of state, but we still keep in touch. We lost one special friend, Robert (O'Bob), who passed away in January of 2016. We are very thankful for all the family and friends we have. We just keep going along.

My struggles paid off, and I'm very fortunate I had so many people along the way to help me. At my age now (seventy-five), it's not that important to me anymore to get my GED in the traditional way. I feel I did get my GED the practical way, through hard work and perseverance. I am happy just knowing things are now better. I decided I'm not going back to school, although I did enjoy it. I can practice reading anywhere.

My years spent in grade school were a disaster. I don't know where I got my confidence from, what kept me going, and what kept me out of big trouble. So many times, I felt so lost and desperate and had a very low feeling of self-worth. But there were so many good things in life, they made up for it. It seemed something always came my way that made me feel good. I did at times think, *Why me?* But then again, there were enough good things in life, so I tried to push that self-pity away. I just knew I had to try a little harder. After all, this was the only place I could be, so I knew I may as well try to feel happy and accept that I was doing my best. After going to the College of DuPage later in my life and accomplishing what I did, I feel very confident, and I'm so thankful for all the help I got along the way.

I thank my teacher, Renai Graham, so much for her patience and perseverance in giving all her students the knowledge to conquer the difficult task of learning to read. More importantly, I believe she instilled a great pride in us for our accomplishments. Over the many years spent in the classroom, Renai was a truly dedicated teacher.

I realize that at times it must have been a little frustrating to her as well, trying to get some of those many concepts into our heads. Without dedicated teachers like Renai, our school system would be in pretty bad shape. I hope teaching methods have improved over the years and, more importantly, teachers' understanding of "problem" children also have improved. Children cannot learn when they feel embarrassed and are put on the spot. That just makes them feel inadequate and depressed.

I know from firsthand experience what a difference a good and caring teacher can make. I sincerely thank all the good teachers everywhere for helping all our children succeed. All children need to fit in and feel good about themselves. When adults take the time to listen and understand their problems, it makes all the difference in the world. Sincere guidance from caring people can last a lifetime.

I think back to the beginning. When did I become aware that I was a person? Maybe when I was four or five years old, when I remembered I was hurt, hungry, or happy. What are the memories that mean the most to all of us? Certainly we don't want to remember being hurt, but it is always there. We remember being hungry, and that does pass, but most of all, I think we remember people caring about us, loving and protecting us, and being proud of our accomplishments. And, more importantly, we remember being kind to and taking care of those we love.

I am so appreciative for the opportunity given to me to be on *The Oprah Winfrey Show*, where I was able to express the difficulties of having dyslexia. Illiteracy is by no means a new subject, and the fact that it was discussed on national television, and I was so personally involved with the show, makes me so very proud. The TV network did a great service to those in the viewing audience who may have similar issues. Hopefully they benefited from these shows, and they know that they are not alone.

During the show, I had the great privilege of meeting and talking with Dr. Phil McGraw and he offered me some words of wisdom. Dr. Phil has a daily TV show that my wife and I enjoy watching. We find his program very powerful and of extreme importance on so many subjects. Through his show, he offers urgent assistance to so many hurting people. What an honor it was to meet him in person!

I also sincerely thank Oprah Winfrey for being a great humanitarian and giving all her guests on that millennium show the opportunity to share each of their very personal issues with millions of viewers. All the hopes and goals of the guests were important, and their stories were very moving.

There were some teachers along the way that helped me in some way. They may not have understood exactly what was holding me back, but their kindness really helped. Also, I had many friends as well as family members, who were very patient with me and overlooked some of my obvious flaws. That really helped me to carry on and feel good about myself.

Needless to say, I thank my wife, Bonnie, and my daughter, Jackie, so very much. Bonnie has been right alongside of me throughout the many years we've been together and continues helping me along. I'm just glad it turned out that way. When it came right down to getting back to school, Jackie motivated me to try just a bit harder. She helped me get into the College of DuPage for the adult literacy classes and provided a path to be able to participate in Oprah's show.

I would like to again mention my friend Joe. He has been, and will always be, a very good friend of mine. He has helped me in so many ways. I still remember the day I first met him; I was a new employee at Illinois Tool Works. It took about a year before I felt I really got to know him. At that time, he introduced me to a lot of people, especially the bosses. This helped me feel very important and comfortable with ITW management.

Joe didn't know I had a reading problem, and I certainly was not going to give that away. He was able to help me with my job just by talking. After two or three years, we started to work on automobiles. He taught me a lot about cars, and I got pretty good as an auto mechanic. We could fix almost anything.

If it weren't for Joe, I never would have gotten so far. Of all the people I could have met at my job, I was very fortunate that Joe was that person. I am so thankful for our friendship. He has taught me more than just how to work on cars. He has taught me about working on houses, too. Electrical, plumbing, tiling, putting up plasterboard—you name it, Joe can do it. Joe is truly my mentor, and to this day, I still call him for advice.

Joe and I have been good friends for over fifty years and I kept my secret from him most of that time. After I went to school, I finally told him that I could now read. When he found out, he asked why I didn't tell him sooner and said he could have helped me. He had no idea how much he really had helped me already. So many people were totally surprised. And after the Oprah show, there was no hiding anymore. I was very proud to have finally admitted I carried this problem around and I was overcoming it.

It's hard to put into words how fortunate I am that I had, and still have, the support of my family and friends. I could not have done this alone.

REFERENCES

Freire, Paulo and Macedo, Donaldo. 1987. Literacy: *Reading the Word and the World*. Westport, CT: Bergin and Garvey.

Lee, Harper. 1960. *To kill a mockingbird*. Philadelphia: Lippincott.

Wilson Language Training Corp. 1998, Fall/Winter. Wilson on prime time with Oprah and Al Lewis! *The Decoder 8* (1): 5, 12.